BURN

Crab Orchard Series in Poetry
Editor's Selection

BURN

SARA HENNING

Crab Orchard Review &
Southern Illinois University Press
Carbondale

Southern Illinois University Press
www.siupress.com

27 26 25 24   4 3 2 1

The Crab Orchard Series in Poetry is a joint publishing venture of Southern
Illinois University Press and *Crab Orchard Review*. This series has been made
possible by the generous support of the Office of the President of Southern
Illinois University; the Office of the Vice Chancellor for Academic Affairs
and Provost; and the School of Literature, Writing, and Digital Humanities
in the College of Liberal Arts at Southern Illinois University Carbondale.

2022 Crab Orchard Series Editor's Selection
Editor of the Crab Orchard Series in Poetry: Allison Joseph
Jon Tribble, series founder and editor, 1998–2019

Cover illustration: Flame of burning alcohol by Volha Kliukina. Adobe Stock
image #263308810, image has been cropped.

Library of Congress Cataloging-in-Publication Data
Names: Henning, Sara, author.
Title: Burn / Sara Henning.
Other titles: Burn (Compilation)
Identifiers: LCCN 2023028106 (print) | LCCN 2023028107 (ebook) |
ISBN 9780809339280 (paperback) | ISBN 9780809339297 (ebook)
Subjects: LCGFT: Poetry.
Classification: LCC PS3608.E564536 B87 2024 (print) |
LCC PS3608.E564536 (ebook) | DDC 811/.6—dc23/eng/20230626
LC record available at https://lccn.loc.gov/2023028106
LC ebook record available at https://lccn.loc.gov/2023028107

Printed on recycled paper ♻

SIU
Southern Illinois University System

In memory of Jon Tribble (1962–2019)

What will become of you and me
(This is the school in which we learn . . .)
Besides the photo and the memory?
(. . . that time is the fire in which we burn.)
—Delmore Schwartz, "Calmly We Walk
through This April's Day"

As we shall see, the concept of time has no meaning
before the beginning of the universe.
—Stephen Hawking, *A Brief History of Time*

Time is the longest distance between two places.
—Tennessee Williams, *The Glass Menagerie*

CONTENTS

I.

Galveston, Texas   3
Stealing *Ariel*   5
Good Kissing   7
A Brief History of Fathers   9
Letter in the Shape of a Banyan Tree   11
Ghost Story   13
Blue   15
Cornfield Elegy   16
A Brief History of Light   17
Almost Men   19
Ars Poetica after an Abnormal Mammogram   21
Olives   23
Year of the Horse   24

II.

A Brief History of Fire   29

III.

The Virgins' Club   45
When I Choose a Man   46
Cairns at School House Beach   47
Cat State   48
Texas Duplex   50
Meditation at Panda Express   51
Christmas Quarantine   53
After Uri   55
A Brief History of Hurricanes   56
A Brief History of Skin   58
Drive-In Nights   60
The First Years   62
Men of the Sea   63
Burn   66

Acknowledgments   69
Notes   71

BURN

I.

It made her wonder if hell was a pretty place too.
—Toni Morrison, *Beloved*

GALVESTON, TEXAS

When Brown Pelicans torpedo
the Texas coast, flare their gular pouches

to sieve for prawns, they look
like bombs falling from the sky.

Tell me that the world is on the verge
of ending, and I'll believe you.

Wings clenched to plunge,
like guns, they unfurl for the cock.

Sea-shocked, I watch them cull
through spume, seize up kill.

In a moment's flash, they rise
back to the world of the living.

Since noon, they've slashed past
my condo's glass. Even the wind

seems complicit, brutalizing dunes,
whipping away umbrellas shanked

into sand. *Pod, squadron, fleet*—
such warlike names for creatures

who loiter in the shallows like yachts.
I don't want the miracle of a hunt

to end at the surface, the way time
or pelican arrows its hunger into any

wave's brine-bruised crest. It is nearly
evening. Tell me prawn shell

pried open resembles a heart
and I'll believe you. Pelicans,

they dive as if they have nothing,
everything to live for.

STEALING *ARIEL*

What had I become the night I dreamed
I shot my mother's Smith and Wesson pistol?
I'd never held an oil-slick metal barrel,
fingered the grip of a powerful god.

I only dreamed I shot my mother's pistol,
but my aunt's man told police I cased his Jeep.
Seventeen, I'd never fingered the grip of a powerful god.
Under his grin, his vowels are bitter sugar.

He told the cop on call I cased his Jeep.
Loosened a lug nut. Ice-picked his tire.
Under his grin, his vowels are bitter sugar.
She tried to kill my wife, he said. *She'd kill.*

He said, *She ice-picked my tire—*
His lies, stiff as gin in the morning.
She tried to kill my wife, he said. *She'd kill.*
He hated my mother, which meant he hated me.

His lies, stiff as gin in the morning.
Lights from the cop's car glinted and burned.
He hated my mother, which meant he'd hurt me.
The cop looked at me like one of his daughters.

Lights from the cop's car glinted and burned.
Last week, I'd stolen my mother's copy of *Ariel*.
The cop looked at me like one of his daughters.
My aunt's man said, *Honey, your life is over.*

I thought of Sylvia Plath, her lines
Your body. / Hurts me as the world hurts God.
Your life is over, the cop said,
if you call my station again.

Your body. / Hurts me as the world hurts God.
I'd never held an oil-slick metal barrel.
If you call my station again, he said.
What had I become that night? I dreamed.

GOOD KISSING

After Jorie Graham's "Two Paintings by Gustav Klimt"

The moon, the river bleeding out its glamour
and spume—I wanted to marry it all.
Mosquitoes circling nests of eggs,
dragonflies feasting from dusk-blurred water.
Why did no one teach me that behind
every miracle is a god taking everything
it wants? I'd trace my finger over
the picture book drawing of the tree
of the knowledge of good and evil,
savor the stories of women. *Proverbs*—
Eve, the apple luscious as her sin. *Genesis*—
Lot's wife's a salt goddess, her body
no Sodom, torched. Salome. Delilah.
Potiphar's wife. Jezebel. But when Robert,
my aunt's boyfriend, bomber jacket
hugging his biceps, edged my aunt against
the sink as she sliced tomatoes,
kissed her with an open mouth? I'd never seen
a man touch a woman like that—
his throat flushed, her bleached Farrah
Fawcett cut catching in his mouth.
She gasped, laughed, begged him to stop.
Because I believed he was killing her,
I ran at him, fists raised. A humid afternoon
in Georgia, 1989. Even now, I want
to erase Robert's hands from her body—
his touch proving I was stupid to love's hunger.
Good kissing, my aunt said, is what a man
and woman do to make a baby.
Weeks later, she's pregnant when they go
to dinner, hostess seating them in their favorite
booth. The walls a montage of Elvis EPs—
"Love Me Tender," "Viva Las Vegas."

Photos of the King sealed under
lacquer, the table's scratched history.
For women in my family, every
miracle begins with a man, an origin story.
When she told him, he threw down
twenties, walked straight into the night.
No longer body but shadow of court
hearings, custody payments,
he was the hole her daughter
would learn to call *father*.

A BRIEF HISTORY OF FATHERS

When she speaks of her father, slurs burn my other aunt's throat.
Anger corrodes her chest: *That son of a bitch*, before he was *father*

who left in the night. Husband home late from the rails,
his body so slapped through with coal and sweat his wife

took a broom to the bedsheets. He glimmered, dark diamond,
when the moon flooded their bed. This was before the babies

came, seven of them, like honeysuckle in every corner
of the yard, or the booze, leggy women who'd do anything

for whiskey or nickels to slip into the jukebox. When he stopped
coming home, my grandmother put stones in the soup,

hunted ditch weed, prayed the Nicene Creed. She waited
for Mary to call to her through cracks in her kitchen ceiling.

Once the eviction notices came, she gave her children
back to God. My father learned to slip through the windows

of Saint Vincent's, away from the Sisters, curl on his mother's
porch to sleep. After the death certificate—*heart attack,*

male, fifty-four—my father hitched in the night, never found
a grave. He died there, the boy my father was, hunting

ghosts. My half-brother and I like deep cuts,
blunt as his other scars: nose sliced clean by a shovel,

the bullet he took in Vietnam. Ship fires blazing through
dream rivers, Cong firing shots. LSD chased with one-night

stands. Saint Augustine said we are *united by the common*
object of our love. I read of Pablo Picasso,

his light-scorched centaur, proof that a man
sears his story into the dark. When my father died—

Nickels in the jukebox. Honeysuckle in the yard.
Like his father, he's dead man, dead beat, gone.

LETTER IN THE SHAPE OF A BANYAN TREE

> *I always felt like a bird blown through the world.*
> *I never felt like a tree.*
> —May Swenson, "Stripping and Putting On"

A year before my birth, Mother, you wished for a son to grow inside you. You'd
     call him

banyan tree, strangler fig, boy strong as my father. When I came, you knew

a chickadee starving for love could carry no legacy. Call me

daughter who names creatures of the night like firstborns, daughter persuaded

everything she loved could kill her—possums hissing, their luminous, naked tails.

For consolation, you dressed me in pink, tried to make me your perfect

girl. But I was a tomboy, skinned knees and tangled

hair. Mornings, you'd smoke while braiding me, smooth elastic,

Indigo Girls on the radio. Around my body, the ghost of a son grew.

Jealous, I butchered my Barbies with scissors, played Atari all afternoon—*Donkey*

Kong, rounds of *Frogger* in my beanbag chair. Sunlight seethed with me,

lasered our duplex windows. Love meant learning to run.

Mother, where does it end, this story of us?

Nightmares remind me you've been gone seven years.

Only now, my prayers are bioluminescent, tractor beams luring your ghost

planet back. But my memory keeps you breathing,

quiet metronome for cicadas flexing their tymbals in the yard. I still talk to you

relentlessly, fevered questions about bodies, children,

secret blood that won't stop. When will you answer? Aristotle said

time is how we position ourselves relative to change, but I want to believe any

universe flexes like *Heteractis aurora*, turquoise Beaded Sea Anemone. Space only

valley of muscle, and we are the clownfish slipping through each other to another world. What is a day without darkness? When tumors clustered your

X-rays, Mother, you became infinite. I am not

your banyan, but I branch and sow. I'm a bird blown through the world. Call me

daughter,

zeroed. I'll never let you go.

GHOST STORY

Savannah, my mother would say,
*so beautiful General Sherman could not watch
it burn.* Perhaps this is why we stayed

in this city of rain-torched oaks
two years after my father died, Spanish moss
draping the branches like pashmina over

a dead girl's shoulders. Yamacraws
called it *Itla-okla*, threaded it into ropes
or blankets to warm the haunches

of horses. *Barbe espagnole*, French
colonists mocking the beards of Spanish
conquistadors. But when she said it,

my mother, I believed it—*Savannah*,
so beautiful, so beautiful—like that afternoon,
1984, on the baseball diamond,

when I, four years old, clung to Laurie,
Daisy Dukes razored to graze her
freckled thighs. She was Beth's daughter,

thirteen, piercing her ears with ice
and safety pins, and she watched me when
our mothers left us to sip Dos Equis

and smoke Virginia Slims,
to dish about men or the latest of Laurie's
disasters—Laurie, scaling

the downspout from the bathroom
window to meet boys in the backs of cars.
Laurie, slinking upstairs at twilight,

her underwear in her purse. Her red hair,
I remember how it curled against my face
when I wrapped my arms around her.

Some days I traced the dark circles
under her eyes. Laurie, she clings to me
now like Spanish moss, that wet,

heavy hunger. Two days after she went
missing, they found her raped, throat slit,
heart-shaped holes cut into the breasts

of her Pink Floyd T-shirt. A car's
slashed leather, the heat-ripped metal
of a trash can off Tremont

that held her—no one told me
how she left the world. My mother
only said Laurie had *gone away,*

was *never coming back.* Cops
don't find killers, I'd learn too soon,
in cases like this, for girls who scuff

the toes of their sneakers
when they dance or ash a smoke,
Saturday blooming before them like

a heaven that could seize them up—
raped girl, ghost story. Even Sherman
would not burn it down.

BLUE

My year of firsts will always burn bright blue.
I start with Manic Panic, my boyfriend's head in the kitchen sink.
We cruise in cars, Texaco Icees sweet between our knees.
My mother worked doubles and binge-watched soaps.

In the kitchen sink, I dye my boyfriend's hair.
His name is Elijah, Hebrew for *my God*.
My mother worked doubles and binge-watched soaps.
I steal her menthols, nearly fail the SAT.

I date a boy named Elijah, Hebrew for *my God*.
We spend prom night in the back of his Chevy Astro.
He aced the SAT, helped me pass physics.
From him, I learn that heat is a measure of disorder.

We spend prom night in the back of his Chevy Astro,
back when home was a place I couldn't love.
If heat is a measure of disorder, does time exist?
When we get bored, we wander the aisles at Revco.

Home is a city I could never love.
When Elijah's stepbrother raped my friend, I blame myself.
When we get bored, we wander the aisles at Revco.
Back from Basic, he begs for her number. I ink it on his hand.

He raped my friend. I blame myself.
She's married now. Her husband holds her at night.
Back from Basic, a ghost of a brother begs, inks his rage onto women.
She called me after, screaming into the phone.

I'm married now. My husband holds me at night.
Back then, we cruised in cars, Texaco Icees sweet between our knees.
When I call her number, I still hear her screaming.
My year of firsts will always burn bright blue.

CORNFIELD ELEGY

The verb for it is *glossing* his Chrysler down right lacquered up
windows at half-mast like cigarettes tight-rolled into a T-shirt sleeve
the whole rhetorics of it rust then katydids flitting their wings
rhapsodic One of those nights where even the moon *threw a glare*
He was on top of me in the backseat the verb for it is *shot up*
with pollen and I'm the queen bee all heady and flecked
I'm throat-deep in petals and when I said *no* it was like watching
his tires kick up dust in the field and when I said *stop* corn silk
in a hard wind doves thronging it was tree limbs cast in silver
the salt taste of my piety my body filling with pain every time
he breathed I breathed *Please*, he kept saying impossible now
to unhear it this man on top of me the gate to my body opened
I want to tell you a story about the backs of my knees on his shoulders
they were plum-soft I want to start with a body turned interloper
a story that ends with *I'm sorry* a flashback of him crying out
not lasting long a siren of katydids troubling the rocking car
I'll recall his flood when I finally make it to a bathroom
the way his trace of drowned coriander won't leave me for days
that night always ending with *ending with* Why must I continue
to territorialize this memory? To say something about possessing
a thing until it blazes through the dark? To say something
of bending space and time into a hymn of my own? I'm trying
to tell you a story about a man who buried his body in my body
my spine crushed like a bonsai beneath him the verb for it is *glossing*
as in *to luster* as in *to pity* the whole night smooth the moon
shot up with radiance his call like dog song in my ear
his body still in my body as if love is not a weapon
as if love is not a safe word we knowingly brutalize.

A BRIEF HISTORY OF LIGHT

They will always be love letters,
closed caption letters unspooling across
the TV. My mother, hard of hearing,

watched her stories in silence.
Guiding Light, *One Life to Live*,
living room lit by two Tiffany lamps.

Deep-throated wisterias, peonies
etched against cream at the crown,
all of it cast deep flames at the ceiling.

How many times did I stare into
a lampshade, its luster blunted through
coiled bronze wire and blown favrile,

the canopy of glass in rich charade
all night? Just like that, my knees dirt
-smeared again. Braid down my back,

I'm tilling mica from soil at recess,
swearing it would catch fire in my hands.
I imagined angels tunneling through

layers of earth, catching their wings
on oak roots, bricks, and those little wounds
lodging there, waiting for me

to dig them up with sticks. The way it
sieved light through its scratched surface,
nothing could compete, not the Goody's

barrettes I'd spent whole hours unearthing
while other girls lost themselves in games
of freeze tag, not their tortoiseshell glare.

Queen of the hunt, I'd strut the cache
with me wherever I'd go. So when she died,
my mother, I grasped her lamps

as if I were pulling slivers of dirt-rough
mica from the earth, knowing their iridescence
could burn any house down.

ALMOST MEN

When Tucker Bailey took a dump on the windshield
of Jimmy Kline's 1977 Dodge Monaco, a rare
April blizzard unleashed its fury onto the town.
It was like two boys beating ass, how snow sieged
endlessly into diesel pumps at the Texaco.
The sky's heady intensity coming for us all.
And Jimmy, one of those cattle-famous Klines
who thought he shit roses, shot hoops for St. Mary's
with an angel's drop step and dunk—boy exploding
the rim, mad backspin baller. Before the trip to Kansas City
for band recital, he parked at the Texaco like any
other beast in the paint, but not before giving Tucker
a proper goodbye—*watch out for deer*
on your way home, you little bitch. No one could stop
talking about it, the snow, fluorescent lights
dead over diesel pumps, or the moonlight's flash off
Bud Light cans, their dumpster-flung silhouette
lighting up the night. Or how Tucker, drunk,
dropped his drawers—cupping his balls, bracing
for the shock of shit to rush onto the Monaco's salt
-burned hood, flexing his haunches. Tucker using
sun-bleached Kmart ads from the backseat
to smooth it into the glass, so it could freeze,
atom fused to atom, in little swirls. First the cops
came, then the fire department. Jimmy watched
as firemen shot water onto the Monaco's glass,

stifled laughs—*well, you made your bed, boy,*
now you get to drive around in it. And somewhere,
grinning, Tucker relived this moment, one boy using
his body to overpower another. No punches thrown.
No broken jaws. Just Tucker suspended, his naked ass
in the rush of spring snow, hovering there,
his body opening as though leaving one world
for another.

ARS POETICA AFTER AN ABNORMAL MAMMOGRAM

But I've no spade to follow men like them.
Between my finger and my thumb
The squat pen rests.
I'll dig with it.
—Seamus Heaney, "Digging"

He couldn't save her, my great-grandmother,
the surgeon blading breast from its hinge of ribs—
pectoralis major, rectus abdominis. So he
stitched her, cauterized, sheared until

only skin lashed her heart to the world.
Radical mastectomy. Even cut, a woman saves
what she can. Chicago, 1935. In her kitchen,
biscuits bloomed from rationed lard.

Olives salted the soup. Even week-old
beef in a pot of goulash was born again.
As long as sweat from a day's labor
streaked her husband's clothes, his pockets

clinked with cash, she'd slip bowls
to her neighbors' children out of the door.
Winters no one worked, she made sure no child
starved. When it hardened in her breast

like a walnut's husk, doctors could not cut it
out of her, the tumor or how she loved,
stubborn canna lily, language of her blood.
When my gynecologist called eight millimeters

of asymmetry *abnormal density*, I believed
the tissue in my breasts was unfurling into letters,
decoding an origin song. When the technician
angled me, X-rayed my flesh with a magician's

precision, I became one of Duchamp's nudes,
a glimpse of history. Light's fractal. And later,
an ultrasound's sound waves translated
the grammar of my breasts, transducer slick

on my areola, gel the only interlocutor between
my body and what speaks. I have no knife
to follow women like her, my great-grandmother.
I cut with words. I'll feed a city.

OLIVES

Small bitter drupes
Full of the golden past and cured in brine.
—A. E. Stallings, "Olives"

It's the olive tooth

-pick-stabbed, odalisque sleek in

her martini bath

I can't untaste now, olive

soaking her tired body

in Epsom, so bored

she's glamorous. Iced gin, watch

it glisten her, steep

her in its aching mirage.

Like gasoline in hot air,

it kisses her hard.

She's a brine-hallowed goddess

I leave for the end.

Or is she little whale,

her belly soft with yearning?

I can't resist her.

Fallen, pine-brusque, she's calling

from her coup of glass—

olive, thick love. I pluck her

with my fingers. I eat her.

YEAR OF THE HORSE

2006

If I told my man I was born
        in the Year of the Horse, not the Monkey,
                would I have run toward him with the faith

                of a dead broke mare, or would I crush him?
        If I could unspool the years, seventeen of them,
with the trained heart of a mother, could I

save it, little slip of blastocyst hushed up
        in me, murmur of bone and song no bigger
                than an angelfish? If sun tore through

                the pines then like they tear now, winter
        of my forty-third year, would I tell him
I was scared to be a mother when I meant

I was scared of a life without a child
        to save me? Would the persimmon-colored
f   lush of my anger rush through me,

                would I turn away from him as I turned
        away from Lexington, the place we called
home, his battery of words overpowering

my will? Would I angle my heart toward
        a strength beyond what I knew? Or would
                I lean into his chest, trust his clove

                cigarette to turn everything sweet
        as a future without what our bodies,
in their perfect recklessness,

made together? If I told my man
    I was born in the Year of the Horse,
        not the Monkey, would I be a mother now?

II.

Each of us is born with a box of matches inside us but we can't strike them all by ourselves.
—Laura Esquivel, *Like Water for Chocolate*

A BRIEF HISTORY OF FIRE

> *You were my miracle, Gabby. You were my miracle. I love you.*
> —Captain Matthew Casey, *Chicago Fire*

I.

Flames split the walls with a jagged chemical grace.

A body language—metal breathing.

He strips off his mask. He gives up his Halligan bar.

On TV, a wife watches her husband die in a fire.

He repeats her name. Listen, he's calling for her.

What I mean is I'm watching a wife watch her husband die.

He's CBing her through his two-way wireless.

She searches his voice as sparks tongue through his boots,

thinks *hope*, like *hell*, is just a four-letter word.

Like *fire*. Like *fear*. Like *future*, untethered. Like *over*.

I'm watching two voices clash through radio waves:

You were my miracle, when he means every exit is choked.

A husband's last rites as debris dirties the air.

She shushes him as another window explodes.

II.

She shushes him as another window explodes.

Loving a man is loving a body with the threat

of ash all around it—you're his kerosene.

His flash point glimmers when you touch his skin.

But I'm at a safe distance: no smoke in my kitchen.

My husband stretches, dreams in his recliner.

The TV blurs and murmurs in the dim.

Memory guts me open. My father

was a fireman before a fire raged in the house

of the holy. In 1982, lightning

struck the steeple of a Baptist church.

The roof warped and bowed. The ceiling awakened.

Holiness is a force. My mother liked to say

God was inside my father when he died.

III.

God was inside my parents when they caught

the fever of baby-making. Muscled in my mother,

I was a dark *yes*, a seed not a sin. *You don't have a daddy,*

Jess said near the monkey bars, her pretend fuchsia

horse bucking beneath her. *That means you're a bastard.*

Bastard, a word for men who stoked my mother's wrath—

your uncle with his stupid Jesus talk

is a real bastard. My mother's revision—

I took your father to court. You're bona fide.

My defense to trick the low-down dirtiest

of playground girls was heaven-sent—*I'm bona fide,*

but ugly is forever. Jess swore, then told on me.

Later, at lunch, she pissed her pants. *God help*

your britches, I said. *I'm still praying for your face.*

IV.

He gags on ash, coughs, but it sounds like prayer—
remember us happy, together, holding each other.
Flame-lashed stairs crash through the ceiling. There's no
way out. She says, *you find a wall, you break it down.*
It's like I'm watching my father die, his body
unthreading in front of me—a no-good man
in love is a still a man. Goodbye, his aubade
of smoke. He planted babies in women the way
corn slips deep after the sow. He'd stalk
my mother's yard in a broken-down Winnebago.
He'd call from a payphone late at night, high
on tight-rolled hashish. He'd murmur half-truths
into the receiver's click. He'd talk to dead air.
I love you, he said. *I'm going back to my wife.*

V.

I love you, he said. *I'm going back to my wife.*
Wife, as if to say *the heart drags itself home.*
Her name is Myra—dark wedge cut. Her eyes
glazed over in pictures. She's luscious with hurt.
My mother was a place to lay his burden down.
His tall-drink-of-water woman, his devil
woman, his good-time girl. I'm twenty when
I test the word *brother* in my mouth,
spit it at my mother as if to shame her.
Her reply: *Mitchell is two years older than you.*
I drop the phone. Is this my history?
My father's wife. My father's son. Then me,
a cameo in my mother's dream:
I'm laughing, blonde, holding a red balloon.

VI.

I'm laughing, blonde, holding a red balloon,

while Mitchell, a toddler, follows the path of smoke.

Hoses shoot water. His mother speaks to men

in hushed tones. He's chasing a toy train lost

to the gutter's current. All around him, crickets

thrum their wings, their chirrups lacing the dark.

Later I'll read about a parasite—*Ormia ochracea*,

a fly that breaks the cricket's glitz of chitin,

his love cry only code for her to rush the optic lobes

of his brain, to tongue the sleek inner thorax, to lay

her young in the temple she makes of his dying body.

Think of it—stoned on heart blood, your eyes flit open.

What it must be to wake in ecstasy,

that slow, blue hour just before the light.

VII.

He's victim to that blue hour—the TV
husband, I mean. We are back to my hand lingering
in a bowl of popcorn, my face wet with another
woman's tears. Diabetes is the fire churning
in my husband's blood—*mellitus*, Greek, as in *like honey*.
His fate, literally to *siphon*, from *diabainein*,
to *go through*. What does it mean to die of sweetness?
His blood is a story of rust, a boy's clash
with barbed wire, that spring-feral crazy of a child
outrunning his soul. His blood is his story of yearning
stripped to the bone—a mother, then a father.
Hate murmured into sugar when the sugar turns.
When a father leaves, when a mother gives her grief
to her children—it's enough to kill a son.

VIII.

A mother's yearning—it's enough to kill a son.

Ten and she's gliding her stick of Secret roll-on

under his arms, the funk of manhood sprung

like testimony from his pores. This is the year

girls were not cootie queens but a thick

heat dirge in his hips. In rage or vendetta,

he baptizes himself in hot water. He scrubs

and scrubs. This is how a boy arrives

into his shame. Once one man lets go,

another becomes visible. As if to say,

son does not mean *effigy*. Son does not mean

tome of the father, nor does it mean *to listen*

or *to sweeten*. Son does not mean *he who trains*

the dog heart of loneliness to famine and moan.

IX.

To famine or to moan, to bay or to kindle, a boy
is a rogue ship drifting through his mother's moods.
He slips and pivots, pirate child, another
man of war. While his father hauls load, he's man
of the house. A trucker's son. Think of his mother,
the radio's lilt, her signature gravy that could
soothe any afternoon down to the bone—*the goop*,
she called it. Shit on a shingle. Stick to your ribs
kind of grub a man should eat with his sons. Think
of the motel breezeway, not the boy, his mother casing
his father's parked truck. It happens fast—heat
through a flung-open metal door. His father in sheets,
then a woman's *oh*. A flash before his memory
blanks. Snow glittering everything that moved.

X.

Snow glittering everything that moved.

The gun-metal white of a mother's rage. Pillow marks

damning her face all winter. Rosacea islands.

Trash bags holding his father's things: Was it stereo

smashed by a baseball bat, scissored-up

Rustler jeans? In the way of the jilted, a boy

becomes man of a house divided. Which is to say

a boy hardens, splits. His mother watches

his body surface, as if from a conspiracy—

his father's muscled shoulders. The same hands.

A mother hugs her boy as if to whisper,

Don't you leave me too. She feeds him her burdens

like potatoes smothered in butter. He swallows her pain.

He jokes, *I'm a sweet kid. I've got the blood to prove it.*

XI.

A sweet kid, with the blood to prove it—*husband*,

must our metaphors for self-destruction

hold the formula for how we grieve?

When we say *son*, do we mean the father

in our blood always leaving? When mothers hate

themselves through their children, could we say

this *motherpain* is transactional,

a honeysuckle vine taking root?

Vicious helix, it twists before it grips.

Is this how women become mothers, our flower

throat fever turning us holy, our hunger for

another woman's son making us say,

Mea culpa? Is it legacy unfurling,

this love, or just another sweet that kills?

XII.

Is love our legacy or does it kill?
Imagine a woman gazing into the flames
of a warehouse fire, her husband trapped inside.
Imagine a woman not exploding with the next
bunker of oil, but losing herself in the most
measured way, her grief so modest it stuns:
Her eyes glitter. Her cheeks glisten with salt.
Imagine a woman who does not keen or sink
to her knees to bargain or to beg, but who holds
her husband's voice like it's his body. Without breaking
the fourth wall, I'm leaping into the hothouse
of another woman's pain. I'm watching a wife
watch her husband die in a fire, which is to say—
She's losing everything she loves.

XIII.

What is a woman when miracle doesn't mean
the roof is coming down? I want to see
a woman, not a fuchsia horse hurtling
past the scrim of memory, not an animal
threshed by the heels of a brutal girl. I'm here
for a miracle, not a cricket lacing the dark
with its solo, not the father in our blood
already gone. If miracle means a mother
has laid her burden down. If husband means
that new blood moan. I'm watching a woman—hear me—
not a *mea culpa*, not a temple
unpetaling. A woman stoned on heart blood
refuses to crystallize. I'm watching her,
vine of honeysuckle, unribbon. Then open.

III.

The heart is the toughest part of the body.
Tenderness is in the hands.
—Carolyn Forché, *The Country between Us*

THE VIRGINS' CLUB

We're a clutch of sophomores still French kissing pillows, zits like stars
in our skin. We pass Oxy 10 like joints between classes. The Virgins' Club—

me, Kim Childers, Madeline Stein. We zip our too-tight jeans with coat hangers,
suck in our guts. We're queens who lick cream from Oreos at lunch. *Virgin*—

like the record label, or a forest never touched by mankind. I watch girls
sneak hall passes, skip class to screw in cars. I'd drink virgin

daiquiris at parties where cool girls play beer pong, make out
with jocks during rounds of spin the bottle. *Virgins make good wives,*

I hear. Kim's first, her boyfriend's figure-four leg lock, like Ric Flair
putting the hurt on the Hulkster. Madeline uses her one-way ticket out of V-Town

on a Brit across the pond. But mine I gift to a physics whiz who
deserts me for tournament rounds of *Minecraft.* If only I'd kept the verb

of my body, that mother of pearl, hushed in my shell. If only
I'd marry myself. Who doesn't want a virgin, after all?

At thirty, I'll meet you, man who takes me to bed and means it.
On our wedding night, I know I'll never be virgin again.

WHEN I CHOOSE A MAN

July is the season of backyard barbecues, slabs of ribs bone-down and sluicing,
citronella kissing through me like a mosquito's sting. Around me, men flaunt
flip-flops and aloha shirts, their tank tops inked with sweat. They don't resemble
men I chose years ago: the chef moving through me like he's skinning a salmon
barehanded, his touch leaving me wound-naked, radiant as a cat in heat. I still
fantasize about the way a hip-shaped bottle of Malbec turned his lips the color
of my hunger. Or the railroad man who slow-danced me in snakeskin boots
to George Strait, his cocktail of Stetson and greased-up Levi's still deep in my
sheets. When I choose a man, he will have scarred his hands working quarry to
put himself through college, ghosts of calluses still churning in his palms. When
I choose a man, he will have our children, unborn, lurking in his blood. He will
angle his head in my lap and, half asleep, whisper—*I am home.*

*

Love erases youth,
        that ephemeral wreck. O
husband, take me home.

CAIRNS AT SCHOOL HOUSE BEACH

Washington Island, Wisconsin

At Boyers Bluff, limestone glints like peach pits at water's edge. We
bathe where sun lashes Lake Michigan like Courbet's *La Brême*, that Realist

requiem of light. This bluff's a dried-out sea carved by glacial force. Cool
to the touch, water is the god binding us to surf zone. The beach, we

learn, was formed by *littoral drift* as wave-whipped slabs eroded. What's left
is muscled-down rock. Families swarm each summer to hunt schools

of yellow perch littering the surface like tourmaline. But we
are here to build cairns, to Jenga rock into little fortresses. I lurk

the shore for the best shards to lattice into design. Late
after lunch, I find thick-bellied queens, gleaming cat's eyes. We

call ourselves architects of swash, while near us, a father strikes
a bet with his son. Who skips the best rock wins. The boy aims straight,

hustles his angles. They take turns trawling, talking smack. We
tried three years—tracked ovulation, peed on hCG strips. Now, I single

out rocks like a mother, learn to haunt beaches where the sin
of my body, like lime, is lovely wreckage. Close to sunset, we

linger at the dock in Adirondack chairs, hold hands as dusk thins
the sky to a hush of bruises. Pelicans preen, dip as I sip gin,

imagine the sky is fire. Somewhere, a fish boil plumes and spits. We
hunger for the scent of whitefish knifed from bone. Somewhere, a jazz

band throats deep blue. It is almost perfect—Wisconsin in June,
yachts in the harbor, Montmorency cherries ripe for the pluck. We

take the night ferry past Plum Island Lighthouse to cross Porte des Morts.
I think of my cairns, how soon I fell to my knees in the water.

CAT STATE

It's true, my mother-in-law said. *The boys
from Carthage High School came with their guns.*

The biology class project was to dissect a cat,
to learn the structure of an animal's organs.

A girl from class offered up her family's barn
ferals, mousers who mated in the piss-striped rafters,

fur mangled by fights and wood ticks. It took
the boys an hour to shoot, then load the bodies

into the cargo bed of a borrowed farm truck,
drive to the high school where the teacher waited

to skin and tag them. The girl who offered them
didn't know her pet tom was in the barn

that morning, called by hunger or the queens
in heat. But she knew him, naked, splayed ventral,

his islands of muscle sheathed under skin.
I imagine boys, oblivious, teacher dismissing

the rest of class, girl cradling what was left
of her heart in a towel. As she told this story,

my mother-in-law, she laughed the laugh
of a woman whose father found cattle dead

in the winter switchgrass, who knew what
it meant when locusts come. In physics

class, years ago, while I struggled to calculate
the speed of light, I'd think of Schrödinger—

boxed cat, poison flask, radioactive atom.
I didn't know what it meant when my teacher

said radioactivity is a quantum process,
that a cat could be both alive and dead.

The experiment, he said, is theoretical, a study
in superposition. But I can't stop thinking

about the cat hissing in the dark, spraying
urine in sleek arcs. How it must bunt its head

until blood comes, slash through wood
with its claws. I wanted to ask my teacher

to chalk the equation of survival onto
the board. I want to know if the cat ran

from the high school boys or if, purring,
he rubbed his haunches against their knees.

The girl, I'm still falling into her story—
my hands, wood-blistered, circle a shovel.

I plant the cat in the soil like a field
of pasqueflower, dark lavender flaring after

months of ice. In my dreams, it blooms
like anything loved enough to live again.

TEXAS DUPLEX

Nacogdoches

Darkness was upon the face of the deep.
It seethes through ice-clenched pines, then shakes the stars.

I seethe through ice-clenched pines, shook
by the fractal of needles knifing my roof.

A fractal of needles knifes my roof.
My neighbor's generator throats its song all night.

Legend says only in death, a swan will throat its song.
Here is my song: *no heat, no water.*

No heat, no water. No water, no heat.
The spirit of God moved upon the face of the waters.

I boil snow, see the face of God.
I ask, *how many children froze to death last night?*

How many children must freeze to death tonight?
Texas, so deep in darkness I wear its face.

MEDITATION AT PANDA EXPRESS

My rendezvous begins at Panda Express,

slinking between slivers of cabbage. Orange

chicken's opulent flame bewitching my fork.

Crab rangoon is a star-shaped pleasure

boat, princely lady-killer of salt.

I'll slide through cheap red oyster pails, night

wishes for dim sum, this sorry effigy. I've learned to love nights

in parking lots—Panda Express,

its marquee at the drive-through exalting

the stars. I want this bear-shaped oracle

to shepherd me, to ease

the grief I now mistake for hunger. I focus

on freeing my fork

from its plastic, hold it up to the light.

On nights like this, the sky is shattered blue. *Please*,

my prayer to no one. *X's. O's. X's.*

Saturdays, husband, we used to split an Orange

Julius, suck until we could taste each other's salt.

We'd summer in beachside condos, sip salt

-rimmed margaritas. Now, I fake

joy when you won't look at me. *Orange*

you glad I didn't say banana? I joke. Nights,

you're no better than a ghost. *I think I'll pick up Panda Express,*

I say. You nod. These days, I learn to please

myself. My headlights rapture shadows. *Please,*

I say, searching for my face in the salt

-kissed streets. It is winter. I want my mother, her *yes*

to everything: drive-through cruising, forking

through lines. *Our night drives,*

she'd call them. Dying, I'd feed her orange

slices between hits of morphine. Orange

rind, Orange Julius, orange you glad I didn't say—*Please*

don't go. Now, I do the leaving. Night

is only darkness, reimagined. Salt

where longing existed. Scar-shaped fork.

My rendezvous begins at Panda Express.

Orange chicken, a better man's swagger of salt.

I begin with *please*, ask for an extra fork.

Tonight, at Panda Express, I'll eat my heart.

CHRISTMAS QUARANTINE

When oak limbs gut my mother's axle, she's speeding.
Rain. Fog. Seventy on Simonton Bridge Road.
She stutters the brake against the coming shunt—tires
churned open, sidewalls debeading from each rim. She called it
Murphy's Law, when tires unbelt from steel.
Knees down, she tracks her Motorola flip phone

through dirt pools, torn fast-food bags. The phone
still rings. Christmas 2005, and my mother speed
-dials me from Georgia, as though my voice can steal
her back from night's holdup. *Every road
ends in disaster*, she says. Fate's callboy
screwing her over. *Christmas*, she says, tires her—

so many trees tinseled with ghosts. Her spare tire
won't last thirty miles. She exhales cigarette smoke into the phone.
This Christmas, I get another kind of call—
my husband lunched with someone sick. Coronavirus, speeding
through breath, hangs in the air. Some animal rode raw
and mean. We're contact traced. I steel

myself for the reckless weather of tests, the way steel's
amplitude submits to frost or burning. I'm this tirade
of physics, quarantined. My body a road
converging. I don't expect to hear the phone
ring on Christmas Day, a nurse's voice speeding
through diagnosis: COVID-negative. Her callous

rush of syllables clip and drawl. They're a calling

card, lovely and crude as my mother's steel

-blue eyeliner, spritz of musk perfume. The speed

of longing glazes everything I touch. Tired,

I put a record on. Vince Guaraldi's piano

rekindles my memory of Charlie Brown. I ride

the slur of arpeggios like my mother rides

the shoulder of Simonton Bridge, already stranded, calling

my name. Rain. Fog. A shattered flip phone

glitzing through mud. Memories like steel

undulant in their shame. *I'm tired*

is the heart of any elegy. Grief's speedometer,

tires lashing. It's Christmas again. My mother's dead.

The cry of the piano lurks in the air, steals

its way into me. It rides my body home.

AFTER URI

The earth is dry and they live wanting.
Each with a small reservoir
Of furious music heavy in the throat.
—Tracy K. Smith, "Duende"

April's a tirade of lightning storms. Even the dirt ends up hurting. Everything wants to fight or make love. So when the amaryllis came from the mail order catalog, it came in darkness, wrapped in plastic's tourniquet. I wanted its bloom to wake me, save me, so I set it outside, not expecting the sky to break. When the power grid crashed, all I yearned for was light. I snaked cords through the dining room window, the mechanical yawp of a borrowed generator hammering my patio's brick. There were runs on water, runs on gas. When rolling blackouts fried the surface water plant, I caught droplets in pots, used my propane grill to boil away bacteria. Thieves placed skimmers where I swiped credit cards. I mistook ice-cracked branches slapping ground for gunshots. Linemen worked through the night. When the lights flashed on, I was a ghost returned to my body. So when the amaryllis came, not yet flaring its blood-red petals, I knew how to wait for a soul to come home. I watched the bulb breach, unleash its furious music.

A BRIEF HISTORY OF HURRICANES

As Hurricane Laura raged toward the heel
    of Louisiana's boot, we watched a coroner wheel

      our neighbor out of his front door on a gurney.
        With his body went the whole alphabet of the world.

We stood there, husband, staring through blinds,
    embarrassed we didn't know his name. The stars,

      they're dead before their light ever reaches us.
        His living room, dark save for a single torchiere,

its sprawl of glow bleeding out. I want to know why
    darkness can be interrupted by the idea of a star,

      as if time never existed. Time, it slips within me—
        my mother's blood, my father's blood, blood

of a whole generation—that furious haunting.
    My aunt's double-wide clutched up by Hurricane

      Andrew. My mother planking windows
        to quash the electric hymn of water, skin,

David shelling Savannah with my father's fury.
    You stayed up, husband, waiting for the strike—

      horror, water, an eye that spares us.
        But I'm lost in sleep's turbine, images

of our neighbor spliced against my aunt's schnauzer,
    the one she left in a moment's flash,

      hurling his scrawny body at their trailer's door.
        I wonder if she's haunted by his bark

twisting through metal as her children
    sprint for the car, no room for him among

    heaps of clothes, Wolf chili cans, wedding photos,
        piles of what she could carry.

In my dream, my neighbor has risen above
    the rage of any water.

A BRIEF HISTORY OF SKIN

> *In the infinite meadows of heaven,*
> *Blossomed the lovely stars, the forget-me-nots of the angels.*
> —Henry Wadsworth Longfellow, *Evangeline: A Tale of Acadie*

Return it, the moles constellating my right shoulder,

deep brown poultice. My husband once kissed

his way into its world. Bless it, biopsy knife

swiping through my flesh, my faith. Unname it

Nevus spilus, little Andromeda galaxy stretching my skin,

its infinite halo of dark matter. Unwhisper the word

melanoma, those sleepless weeks I swore

it glimmered, debris from an exploded star.

Unclench my hand from its jigger of vodka,

uncurl my husband's touch from my shoulder.

Unwhisper the words *cancer, mother.*

Unburden my skin from the blazing Utah May,

where, one spring, the sun ravaged me.

Untangle me from recklessness, untruss

the tumors from my mother's blood.

Return her record player's needle shirring

through scarred vinyl, Mick Jagger throating

blues through her house on Victory Drive.

Rebridle her hair to its messy knot,

unveil the dime-sized mole on the back of her neck.

Give them back, my father's words for it—

forget-me-not of the angels, plush field of stars.

Give her back her body when she still loved

my father, when I still moved within her.

But if you can give me nothing, God,

return her name for me—little one,

infinite meadow of heaven.

DRIVE-IN NIGHTS

> *you know love when you see it,*
> *you can feel its lunar strength, its brutal pull.*
> —Dorianne Laux, "Facts about the Moon"

The drive-in at the A. L. Mangham Jr. Regional Airport is mercy

tonight. Films projected on the side

of a plane hangar. We angle our Subaru, hitch

past rows of F-150s, that haze of silver and red. We kill

the headlights. Tonight, its *Die Hard*, Bruce Willis firing

through radios tuned to 90.1 FM. The moon

could hang a convict, how it churns and glows. The moon

could raise us up in the image of its mercy.

Who would save us now? We pop the hatchback, fire

off the engine as John McClane and Holly side

-eye each other at Nakatomi Plaza. Winter-killed

fields behind us once held bluebonnets. I hitch

up my heels on the dash as John cops a look—hitching

off shoes to fix his nerves, he could be Armstrong walking on the moon.

I can't resist a man who'd kill

for his woman, a Johnny-come-lately who mercies

no one. I married you, husband, when you side

-swiped my heart. Terrorists fire,

take hostages. Hans Gruber calls shots. Once, we caught fire

when we touched. In the fury of summer, got hitched.

We've fought, loved, made up in continuous cycles. It side

-saddled us, our hysterics. The moon,

like Jesus, wept. Watching old movies in the dark is no mercy,

just a mercy that saves us.

But John McClane? He kills

his way back: Beretta 92F, his voice over wire—

Yippie-kai-yay, Motherfucker! when he means *mercy,*

call me home. I know that bait and switch, that flint hitch.

I see it when I take off my clothes—*moon*

in my skin, you call it. *That spectral heat*. My side

of the car is cold. Even longing takes sides.

Husband, is this the life we hoped for? Would you kill

any crook who'd dare touch me? Would the moon

in your gun turn to blazing halo? Let's fire

off hope like a fatal bullet. Let's get hitched

again. Any merciful

justice of the peace must side with fire

when he sees it. Let's kill the lights. Let's hitch ourselves to mercy.

We'll make the moon our savior tonight.

THE FIRST YEARS

Locals call it *the gates of hell*, crater
in the Turkmenistan desert burning

forty years. The longest-burning fire began
six thousand years ago—an Australian

coal seam in New South Wales ignited by lightning,
smiting the biome into barren trails.

But I always come back to the coal seam
blazing under Centralia, Pennsylvania,

where a trash fire plumed against veins of earth.
Since then, it razors through mines, sixty years

feeding on bituminous coal. This is us,
love, hitched at our flash points, flaming head of us

lit incandescent. We are soot torching
ultraviolet, photon emissions burst

from atoms. We wear each other's infrared bands.
In outer space, any flame turns to blue sphere.

But here, our first year, we radiated white.
Rages birthed divorce threats, smelted into sex.

Now, we are flameless combustion, licked flint,
divine red. Love exists in spite of us.

MEN OF THE SEA

is it right
to call them creatures,
these elaborate sacks
of nothing?
—Mark Doty, "Difference"

I had no name for it,
moon jellyfish incognito
among the klatch

of *Stomolophus meleagris*,
gentle bloom of mushroom
-headed medusas blistering

in the sun. My teacher told us
to watch out for sea wasps,
tentacles like a drain

strung with our mother's
hair, not the plate-size drifter,
secret save for its milky bell,

four horseshoe-shaped
canals tucked there, casting
a lavender sheen.

My foot vibrated shocks
of pain as my teacher swabbed
vinegar and I lit up

the world with my cries.
When the pain stopped,
I joined my classmates

to splash again in water
-soaked dunes, natural surrogate
to our backyard baby pools,

only place on the coast
of Tybee Island safe enough
to wade. Later, at the aquarium,

it isn't stingrays I want,
the electric slip of pectoral fin
I graze at the petting tank,

or hammerhead sharks
clowning the glass. It is jellyfish—
half-floating, half

-humming in shallows,
their breach of ectoplasm,
their bioluminescent flame.

Jellyfish I think of when
my husband and I lie
together, our love

slick in the liminal space
between my legs. When a urologist
discovers a congenital cyst

has left us childless,
and he follows the lobular
planes of my husband's

testicles with a wide-bore
needle to prove the existence
of life inside of him,

it could be jellyfish motile
on the stereomicroscope,
whipping engine born

without brains, blood,
or heart raging in the sea
of his body. I imagine

a force that could block
the cooling pipes of a power
station or burst through

fishing nets. Jellyfish,
fierce man of the sea, who once
burned his hunger through me.

BURN

If middle age has a shape, it would be
the body singing, word by luscious word.
My body's glory caught in my lungs.

If I could, I would uncry myself,
send my body back to my mother's womb,
where my father once signed his name

in blood. I hung there, seam
of cells, fixed to my holy order—love's
microscopic blaze so much like breathing.

My heart, still twined to my mother's.
Her body, it held me like she hadn't given up.
I long to be pulled from my mother

some August long ago and lie on her chest,
naked, cord uncut, hair matted to my skull.
I want to fill again the hollow in my mother

death will not take as its house. Teach me,
body, to unscar what is scarred. To cherish
the uncharitable. My breasts, whipped

philosophers. My eyes, a murder of crows.
My thighs are engines, leave traces of fire
as I rise up. Watch me rise up.

ACKNOWLEDGMENTS

I extend my gratitude to the following journals and anthologies in which earlier versions of these poems first appeared: *Alaska Quarterly Review*, *Baltimore Review*, *Briar Cliff Review*, *Delta Poetry Review*, *diode*, *Mezzo Cammin*, *Moon City Review*, *Oakwood* (South Dakota State University), *Palette Poetry*, *South Florida Poetry Journal*, *Southern Humanities Review*, *Sweet*, *Texas Review*, *Whale Road Review*, and *Wild Gods: The Ecstatic in Contemporary Poetry and Prose* (New Rivers Press).

This book would not exist without the support of Southern Illinois University Press and Marshall University. I offer my appreciation to Allison Joseph, who selected this book as a 2022 Crab Orchard Series Editor's Selection, as well as to everyone at Southern Illinois University Press who helped bring this book to life. I also dedicate this book to the late Jon Tribble, one of the best editors and poets to ever grace this earth. Thank you for being a compassionate, committed champion of poetry. You are dearly missed.

I thank Erin Elizabeth Smith and everyone at the Sundress Academy for the Arts in Knoxville, Tennessee. Many of these poems were first written during the academy's monthly online Xfit workshop series.

I am indebted to Heather Dobbins, whose feedback on many of these poems was constructive and transformative. I am also indebted to Team Lengua—Daryl Farmer, Jim Reese, Lynne Golodner, Jason Heron, Nathan Johnson, Jamie Sullivan, and Stephanie Schultz. Thank you for being a great workshop community. To my Stephen F. Austin State University and Marshall families, thank you so much for your unconditional encouragement and care.

Finally, I offer nothing but love to my husband, Matthew—life with you is fire.

"Stealing *Ariel*" (5): Lines quoted from Sylvia Plath come from her poem "Fever 103°."

"A Brief History of Fathers" (9): The artistic technique of drawing with light, first undertaken when Gjon Mili visited Pablo Picasso in the south of France in 1949, produced a series of photos using a small electric light in a dark room. The most famous "light drawing" from the five-session collaboration, many of which were put on display in 1950 in a show at New York City's Museum of Modern Art, was Picasso sketching a centaur in the air. The line "Like his father, he's dead man, dead beat, gone" models Ada Límon's final lines in her poem "The Dead Boy": "dead boy, / dead boy, and gone."

"Letter in the Shape of a Banyan Tree" (11): This poem's final line echoes the sentiment and construction of T. R. Hummer's poem "Where You Go When She Sleeps," specifically the line "Into itself if you love enough, and will not, will never let you go."

"Ghost Story" (13): Before Savannah's renaissance after the success of John Berendt's bestseller-turned-movie *Midnight in the Garden of Good and Evil*, the city was plagued by violence and poverty. This is the Savannah I knew as home. According to journalist Michael Hirsley, "A Georgia Crime Information Center annual report indicated that the Savannah metropolitan area had the highest crime rate of any Georgia metropolitan areas, including Atlanta, in 1985. . . . The Georgia Crime Information Center report showed a 14 percent increase in serious crimes such as murder, rape and robbery in Savannah from 1984 to 1985" (*Chicago Tribune*, September 4, 1986).

"Cornfield Elegy" (16): The phrase "*threw a glare*" comes from "The Foundry Garden," a poem by Stanley Plumly.

"A Brief History of Light" (17): The discussion of angels owes its inspiration from "Questions about Angels," a poem by Billy Collins.

"Olives" (23): The term "thick love" comes from Toni Morrison's novel *Beloved*. When the character Paul D tells Sethe her love is "too thick," Sethe insists, "Love is or it ain't. Thin love ain't love at all."

"A Brief History of Fire" (29): This crown of sonnets references the final episode (#22) of the fifth season of the television series *Chicago Fire*. It originally aired May 16, 2017. The phrase *"Holiness is a force"* comes from Annie Dillard's "A Field of Silence."

"Cat State" (48): In physics, a cat state refers to an equal superposition of two distinctive quantum states. It is also referred to as Greenberger-Horne-Zeilinger state.

"Texas Duplex" (50): This poem incorporates lines from Genesis 1:2 (KJV): "Darkness was upon the face of the deep. And the Spirit of God moved upon the face of the waters."

"Meditation at Panda Express" (51): This poem's title is modeled after "Meditation at Lagunitas," a poem by Robert Hass.

"After Uri" (55): Winter Storm Uri was an ice storm that took place February 13–17, 2021. It affected much of the United States, northern Mexico, and Canada. Described as an extratropical cyclone, it wreaked havoc across Texas, causing one of the worst power outages in U.S. history.

"A Brief History of Skin" (58): This poem's formal approach (the speaker examining her emotional reaction to a cancer scare by leading the reader through a retrospective gaze into her past and at her mother's death) was modeled after Ansel Elkins's brilliant poem "Reverse: A Lynching."

"Men of the Sea" (63): Many of the jellyfish facts and several descriptions (such as how jellyfish blister in the sun as they dry out) are attributable to Philip Lamb's article "Jellyfish Have Superpowers—and Other Reasons They Don't Deserve Their Bad Reputation" (*Scientific American*, December 12, 2017) and Joseph Richardson's "Tybee Jellyfish" (Tybee Island, September 24, 2021, https://tybeeisland.com /discover-tybee/tybee-jellyfish/).

"Burn" (66): The poem's last cadence, "as I rise up. Watch me rise up" pays homage to Maya Angelou ("Still I Rise") and Alicia Keys ("Underdog").

Other Books in the Crab Orchard Series in Poetry

The Flesh Between Us
Tory Adkisson

Muse
Susan Aizenberg

Millennial Teeth
Dan Albergotti

Hijra
Hala Alyan

*Instructions, Abject
& Fuming*
Julianna Baggott

*Lizzie Borden in Love:
Poems in Women's Voices*
Julianna Baggott

This Country of Mothers
Julianna Baggott

The Black Ocean
Brian Barker

Vanishing Acts
Brian Barker

Objects of Hunger
E. C. Belli

*Nostalgia for a World
Where We Can Live*
Monica Berlin

The Sphere of Birds
Ciaran Berry

White Summer
Joelle Biele

Gold Bee
Bruce Bond

Rookery
Traci Brimhall

USA-1000
Sass Brown

*The Gospel according
to Wild Indigo*
Cyrus Cassells

*In Search of the
Great Dead*
Richard Cecil

*Twenty First
Century Blues*
Richard Cecil

Circle
Victoria Chang

Errata
Lisa Fay Coutley

Salt Moon
Noel Crook

Consolation Miracle
Chad Davidson

From the Fire Hills
Chad Davidson

The Last Predicta
Chad Davidson

Unearth
Chad Davidson

Furious Lullaby
Oliver de la Paz

Names above Houses
Oliver de la Paz

Dots & Dashes
Jehanne Dubrow

*The Star-Spangled
Banner*
Denise Duhamel

Smith Blue
Camille T. Dungy

Seam
Tarfia Faizullah

Beautiful Trouble
Amy Fleury

Sympathetic Magic
Amy Fleury

Egg Island Almanac
Brendan Galvin

Soluble Fish
Mary Jo Firth Gillett

Pelican Tracks
Elton Glaser

Winter Amnesties
Elton Glaser

Strange Land
Todd Hearon

View from True North
Sara Henning

Always Danger
David Hernandez

Civil Twilight
Cynthia Huntington

Heavenly Bodies
Cynthia Huntington

Terra Nova
Cynthia Huntington

*Maps for Migrants
and Ghosts*
Luisa A. Igloria

Zion
TJ Jarrett

Red Clay Suite
Honorée Fanonne Jeffers

Fabulae
Joy Katz

Cinema Muto
Jesse Lee Kercheval

Train to Agra
Vandana Khanna

*The Primitive
Observatory*
Gregory Kimbrell

If No Moon
Moira Linehan

Incarnate Grace
Moira Linehan

For Dust Thou Art
Timothy Liu

Strange Valentine
A. Loudermilk

Dark Alphabet
Jennifer Maier

Lacemakers
Claire McQuerry

Tongue Lyre
Tyler Mills

Oblivio Gate
Sean Nevin

*Holding Everything
Down*
William Notter

*The Kitchen of
Small Hours*
Derek N. Otsuji

American Flamingo
Greg Pape

*Crossroads and
Unholy Water*
Marilene Phipps

Birthmark
Jon Pineda

Fieldglass
Catherine Pond

No Acute Distress
Jennifer Richter

Threshold
Jennifer Richter

*On the Cusp of a
Dangerous Year*
Lee Ann Roripaugh

Year of the Snake
Lee Ann Roripaugh

Misery Prefigured
J. Allyn Rosser

*Into Each Room We
Enter without Knowing*
Charif Shanahan

In the Absence of Clocks
Jacob Shores-Arguello

Glaciology
Jeffrey Skinner

Roam
Susan B. A.
Somers-Willett

*The Laughter of
Adam and Eve*
Jason Sommer

Hinge
Molly Spencer

*Huang Po and the
Dimensions of Love*
Wally Swist

Persephone in America
Alison Townsend

Spitting Image
Kara van de Graaf

Becoming Ebony
Patricia Jabbeh Wesley

Even the Dark
Leslie Williams

*The River Where You
Forgot My Name*
Corrie Williamson

All the Great Territories
Matthew Wimberley

Abide
Jake Adam York

*A Murmuration
of Starlings*
Jake Adam York

Persons Unknown
Jake Adam York